The Amazing Book of

OCEAN LIFE

ARCTURUS

ARCTURUS

This edition published in 2020 by Arcturus Publishing Limited
26/27 Bickels Yard, 151–153 Bermondsey Street,

London SE1 3HA

Authors: Michael Leach and Meriel Lland
Editors: Clare Hibbert and Samantha Hilton
Interior Design: Amy McSimpson and Trudi Webb
Cover Design: Stefan Holliland

ISBN: 978-1-83940-813-7
CH008250NT
Supplier 29, Date 0620, Print run 10417

Printed in China

The Amazing Book of OCEAN LIFE

CONTENTS

Watery World

Water covers more than two-thirds of our planet's surface. Nearly 97 percent of this water is saltwater, with just 3 percent made up of freshwater in rivers, ponds, and lakes. Saltwater fills a vast world ocean, which humans have named as five oceans.

Salty Water

The ocean tastes salty because it contains particles of sodium and chloride. Together, these make sodium chloride, which is better known as table salt. These particles, and other minerals, arrived in the ocean through a process called weathering. As rain falls, it collects carbon dioxide from the air. This gas mixes with the water to make carbonic acid. Acids can wear away materials, so as rainwater runs over rocks, it carries away tiny particles, including sodium and chloride. Rivers and streams carry the particles to the ocean.

The **Pacific Ocean** is both the largest and deepest ocean, with an average depth of 4,000 m (13,000 ft).

The **Arctic Ocean** is almost completely covered by ice in winter.

In Pattani, Thailand, salt is gathered on the beach. When the seawater evaporates, or turns to gas, in the hot sun, it leaves behind the solid salt.

Islands of the Maldives, in the Indian Ocean

AREAS OF THE OCEANS

Pacific Ocean: 168,723,000 sq km (65,144,000 sq miles)

Atlantic Ocean: 85,133,000 sq km (32,870,000 sq miles)

Indian Ocean: 70,560,000 sq km (27,243,000 sq miles)

Southern Ocean: 21,960,000 sq km (8,479,000 sq miles)

Arctic Ocean: 15,558,000 sq km (6,007,000 sq miles)

Moving Water

Ocean water is constantly moving. As the wind blows across the surface, it whips up waves, which travel right across the ocean until they curl over and "break" on the shore. Currents are great rivers of water that snake around the oceans. Some currents are caused by wind, while others are caused by differences in water temperature. At the surface or closer to the equator, the water is warmer. Warm water rises, while cold water sinks, setting off global movements.

Major currents flow clockwise in the northern hemisphere and the other way in the southern hemisphere. These directions are caused by the turning of the planet, which shifts water and winds to the right north of the equator, but the other way south of the equator.

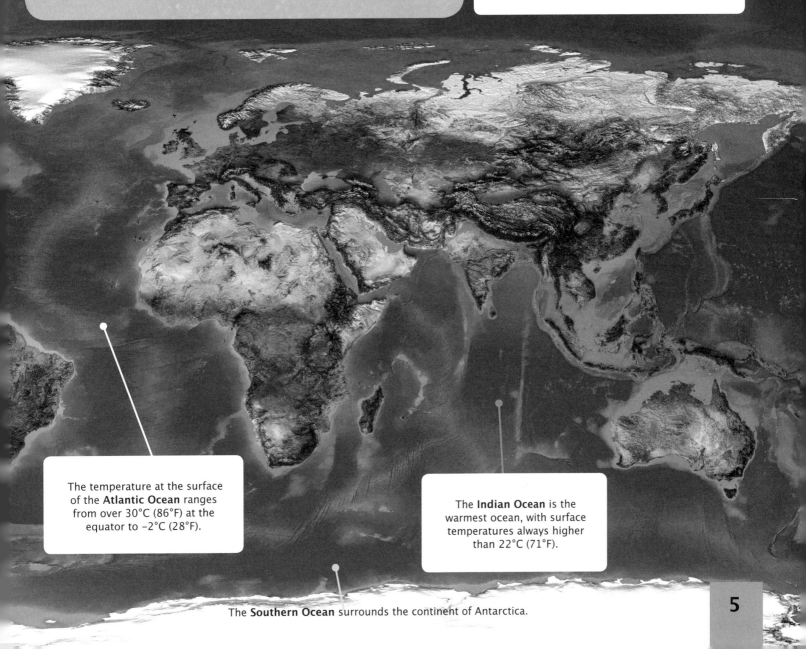

The temperature at the surface of the **Atlantic Ocean** ranges from over 30°C (86°F) at the equator to −2°C (28°F).

The **Indian Ocean** is the warmest ocean, with surface temperatures always higher than 22°C (71°F).

The **Southern Ocean** surrounds the continent of Antarctica.

Ocean Fish

At least 16,000 species of fish live in the ocean. Fish breathe by taking oxygen from the water using their gills. Most fish swim by waving their body or tail, while steering with their fins. Many fish, but not all of them, have skin covered in hard plates called scales.

Breathing through Gills

Fish breathe by gulping water into their mouth. Water contains lots of oxygen. The water flows through the gills, which are filled with tiny blood vessels. The blood vessels soak up the oxygen, which the fish's heart pumps round the body. The used water is released through the gill slits.

Fish Features

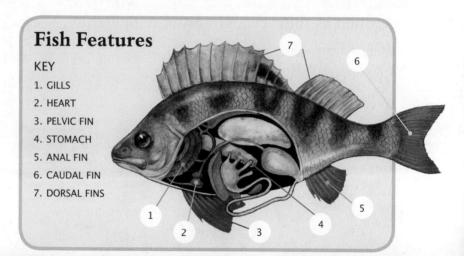

KEY

1. GILLS
2. HEART
3. PELVIC FIN
4. STOMACH
5. ANAL FIN
6. CAUDAL FIN
7. DORSAL FINS

Classes of Fish

There are three classes of fish, which have different body features. The earliest fish to evolve were jawless fish, but most of them are now extinct.

JAWLESS FISH

CHARACTERISTICS:
These fish have no jaws for biting, so they feed by sucking. They have long, scale-less bodies.

SPECIES: Hagfish and lampreys

A lamprey mouth

CARTILAGINOUS FISH

CHARACTERISTICS:
This class of jawed fish have a skeleton made of bendy cartilage. Their skin has many tooth-like scales.

SPECIES: Sharks, skates, and rays

Thresher shark

BONY FISH

CHARACTERISTICS:
These jawed fish have skeletons made of bone. Their scales are usually smooth and overlapping.

SPECIES: All other fish

Yellowtail snapper

MARINE FISH RECORDS

Heaviest and longest: Whale shark, up to 21,300 kg (47,000 lb) and 12.65 m (41.5 ft) long

Longest bony fish: Giant oarfish, up to 11 m (36 ft)

Shortest: Male *Photocorynus spiniceps* anglerfish, as small as 6.2 mm (0.24 in)

Fastest swimmer: Black marlin, up to 105 km/h (65 mph)

Longest living: Greenland shark, possibly up to 400 years

Giant oarfish

Like in other bony fish, the gill slit is protected by a hard cover called the operculum.

The squirrelfish is nocturnal, or active at night. It has large eyes so it can gather as much light as possible.

Pectoral fins, on either side of the head, help with steering.

7

Ocean Mammals

Around 126 species of mammals spend all or part of their life in the ocean. Like other mammals—including humans—these animals need to breathe air, so they come to the water surface regularly. All female mammals feed their young on milk.

Family Life

All marine mammals give birth to live young. Apart from polar bears, which have up to three cubs, marine mammals have just one baby at a time, which they look after for several months or even years. All marine mammals make sounds to communicate with each other, from the songs of whales to the barks of seals.

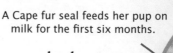
A Cape fur seal feeds her pup on milk for the first six months.

Groups of Marine Mammals

Marine mammals are not all closely related to each other: they belong to different scientific groups with quite different bodies and lifestyles.

CETACEANS

CHARACTERISTICS:
These mammals never leave the water. They have a streamlined body and two limbs that are flippers.

SPECIES: Around 85 whales, dolphins, and porpoises

Minke whale

SEA COWS

CHARACTERISTICS:
Sea cows never leave the water. They have a rounded body and two limbs that are flippers

SPECIES: 3 manatees and a dugong

West Indian manatee

CARNIVORANS

CHARACTERISTICS:
These clawed meat-eaters spend part of their life on land. They have four limbs, which are flipper-like in sea lions, seals, and walruses

SPECIES: 38 sea lions, walruses, seals, otters, and polar bears

Mediterranean monk seal

Atlantic spotted dolphins develop their spots only as they grow older. This mother is fully spotted.

These dolphins communicate with squawks, whistles, and buzzes.

This young dolphin, called a calf, has no spots at all. It will be cared for by its mother for up to five years.

Blue whale

MARINE MAMMAL RECORDS

Heaviest and longest: Blue whale, up to 173,000 kg (381,000 lb) and 33.6 m (110 ft) long

Heaviest and longest carnivoran: Southern elephant seal, up to 5,000 kg (11,000 lb) and 6.8 m (22.5 ft) long

Shortest: Marine otter, as small as 87 cm (34 in) long

Fastest swimmer: Common dolphin, up to 64 km/h (40 mph)

Longest living: Bowhead whale, possibly up to 200 years

Ocean Reptiles

The first reptiles lived on land, but around 299 to 252 million years ago, some reptiles adapted to life in the ocean. Today, there are around 12,000 species of reptiles, but only about 80 are marine. Reptiles need to breathe air into their lungs, so they come to the surface regularly.

Groups of Marine Reptiles

Marine reptiles belong to three orders. The turtle order contains 7 species of sea turtles. The crocodilian order contains 2 species of crocodiles that swim in the ocean. The squamate order contains 1 species of marine iguana and around 69 species of sea snakes. Squamates have skin protected by small, overlapping scales. Turtles and crocodiles grow harder bony plates called scutes.

Like most reptiles, a saltwater crocodile lays tough-shelled eggs on land. To break out of its shell, the baby uses a horny piece of skin on the tip of its snout called an egg-tooth.

Sea Snakes

Of all marine reptiles, sea snakes are best adapted to life in the ocean. While most marine reptiles have to go ashore to lay eggs and perhaps to rest, the majority of sea snakes never leave the ocean. They even give birth to live, swimming young in the water. Only the sea snakes known as kraits go on land to lay eggs.

It kills eels and other fish by biting with its sharp fangs, which inject a dose of venom.

With its paddle-like tail, the ornate sea snake is an excellent swimmer. Although it must surface eventually to breathe, it can absorb some oxygen from the water through its skin.

The yellow-lipped sea krait returns to land to rest, digest its food, and lay eggs.

This sea krait grows to 1.42 m (4.7 ft) long.

A newly hatched leatherback sea turtle makes its way to the sea.

MARINE REPTILE RECORDS

Heaviest and longest: Saltwater crocodile, up to 1,360 kg (3,000 lb) and 6.3 m (20.7 ft) long

Heaviest and longest turtle: Leatherback sea turtle, up to 650 kg (1,430 lb) and 2.1 m (7 ft) long

Shortest: Marine iguana, as small as 29 cm (11.4 in) long

Fastest swimmer: Leatherback sea turtle, up to 35 km/h (21 mph)

Longest living: Saltwater crocodile, possibly more than 100 years

Seabirds

Around 170 million years ago, birds started to evolve from reptiles called dinosaurs. Like most reptiles, birds lay hard-shelled eggs on land. All birds have wings, a beak, and a covering of feathers. Seabirds find their food beaneath the waves, on the ocean surface, or at the shoreline.

Adapted to the Sea

Seabirds have features that help them survive in and around the ocean. Since too much salt is dangerous for birds, many seabirds have glands in their head to remove the salt they swallow while drinking and eating. Seabird wings may be flipper-like for swimming beneath the surface, or extra-wide for flying great distances over the oceans in search of food. Many seabirds have webbed feet, with skin and tissue joining the toes, making them paddle-like for swimming.

The Atlantic puffin dives as deep as 68 m (223 ft) in search of fish. It uses its short, flipper–like wings as paddles, while steering with its webbed feet.

Careful Parents

Seabirds lay fewer eggs than most other birds, many laying just one egg per year. They also spend longer caring for their chicks, with frigatebirds giving the most time—14 months. Seabirds need a different strategy from landbirds because parenting by the stormy sea is dangerous and exhausting, as parents often travel far in search of food for their chicks. By putting all their energy into fewer chicks, hopefully one will survive.

Blue–footed boobies often have two chicks, but the eggs hatch four or five days apart, so the parents do not have two helpless newborns to care for at once.

The white-tailed sea eagle has the largest wingspan (from wingtip to wingtip) of any eagle, reaching 2.45 m (8 ft). It lives around ocean coasts as well as lakes and rivers.

Like other eagles, this bird has a hooked beak for ripping into its prey.

It uses its sharp claws to snatch fish from near the water surface, usually getting only its feet wet.

SEABIRD RECORDS

Heaviest: Emperor penguin, up to 45 kg (100 lb) and 1.3 m (4.3 ft) tall

Largest wingspan: Wandering albatross, up to 3.7 m (12.1 ft) wide

Shortest: Least storm petrel, as small as 13 cm (5.1 in) long

Fastest swimmer: Gentoo penguin, up to 36 km/h (22 mph)

Longest living: Laysan albatross, possibly more than 66 years

Emperor penguins

Ocean Habitats

All living things are adapted to their surroundings, or habitat. In the ocean, the two key things that affect habitat are sunlight and temperature. Animals and plants that live in bright, warm waters could not survive in the darkest, coldest depths.

Temperature Zones

The ocean is warmest close to the equator, where it is heated most strongly by the Sun's rays. All over the world, surface waters are warmer than the waters beneath, as sunlight cannot penetrate farther than 1,000 m (3,300 ft) into the deep.

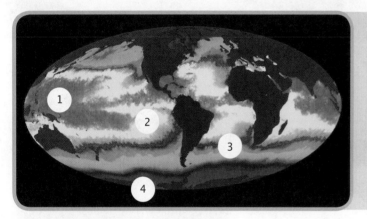

Ocean Climates

This map shows the average temperature at the water surface, from warm (red) to cold (blue).

KEY

1. **Tropical:** Water warm year round
2. **Subtropical:** Water fairly warm year round
3. **Temperate:** Water ranges from cold to warm
4. **Polar:** Water cold year round

Depth Zones

The sunlight zone is rich with life. Plants and single-celled organisms called chromists, make their food from sunlight. These provide food for plant-eaters, which are eaten by bigger species. In the deep dark ocean, there is no plant life and very few animals.

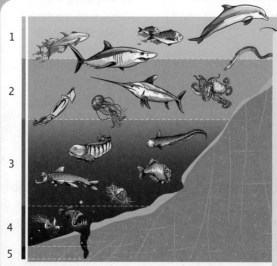

1. **SUNLIGHT ZONE:**
   0 to 200 m (0 to 660 ft)
   Most ocean plants and animals live here.

2. **TWILIGHT ZONE:**
   200 to 1,000 m (660 to 3,300 ft)
   Some animals travel from these dim waters to feed near the surface at night.

3. **MIDNIGHT ZONE:**
   1,000 to 4,000 m (3,300 to 13,000 ft)
   In total darkness, many animals are bioluminescent, or make their own light.

4. **ABYSSAL ZONE:**
   4,000 m (13,000 ft) to ocean floor
   Most animals have special features to survive the cold.

5. **HADAL ZONE:**
   Deep trenches
   Only a few species are known to survive here.

DEPTH AND TEMPERATURE RECORDS

Deepest trench: Mariana Trench, Pacific Ocean, 11,034 m (36,201 ft)

Shallowest ocean: Arctic Ocean, average depth 1,038 m (3,406 ft)

Coldest water: –2°C (28.4°F), Arctic and Southern Oceans

Hottest water: 35°C (95°F), in summer on the coasts of the Persian Gulf, Indian Ocean

Abu Dhabi, Persian Gulf

Many ocean animals are suited to a small range of temperatures and depths. Bigeye tuna are unusual because they can survive in deeper, colder waters and warm surface waters.

The bigeye tuna descends and rises as it follows its prey, such as sardines.

Its large eyes allow the tuna to see when it swims as deep as 500 m (1,650 ft).

Beaches

Sandy or muddy beaches are challenging habitats. Animals and plants must survive being plunged underwater by rising tides and breaking waves, then being exposed to the Sun and wind as the water draws back.

Tides

All beaches have daily high tides, when the sea washes up the shore, and low tides, when the sea draws back out. Tides are caused by gravity. Gravity pulls all objects toward each other, with larger objects, like planets and moons, having the greatest pull. As the Moon pulls on Earth, the sea bulges toward it. As the Earth turns, the moving bulge creates rising and falling tides.

This sand hopper burrows into the sand during high tide, but comes out when the tide is low to feed on washed-up seaweed.

Surviving the Intertidal Zone

Animals living in the intertidal zone, the area between the high and low tide lines, have to survive dramatic changes in their habitat. Some beach animals, such as birds, move up the beach when the tide rises. Others burrow into the sand, choosing wet sand if they need to stay damp. Some insects, such as dune chafer and sandgraver beetles, shelter in the seaweed and driftwood found at the high tide line.

The lugworm burrows in damp sand. It eats sand, digesting the microorganisms it contains, then poops out a coiled "cast" of used sand.

SANDERLING

Length: 18 to 21 cm (7 to 8 in)

Range: Arctic in summer; Americas, Africa, Europe, Asia, and Australasia in winter

Habitat: Sandy and rocky beaches

Diet: Buried invertebrates, including arthropods, mollusks, and worms

Conservation: Not at risk

A sanderling pulls a bloodworm from the sand.

This crab lives on tropical beaches of the Indian and Pacific Oceans.

The horn-eyed ghost crab's eyes are on stalks, which can be folded down when it is burrowing.

The crab uses its claws to burrow into the sand, so it can hide during the day.

Coral Reefs

Coral reefs are rocky ridges built by stony corals. These are animals without a backbone, called invertebrates. They live in large groups called colonies. Reefs are found in shallow, tropical waters. Some coral species live in cold, deep water, but they do not build great reefs.

Building Reefs

Reefs are made of the skeletons of millions or billions of stony coral polyps. A polyp has a soft, cuplike body, armed with tentacles for catching food. Each polyp builds a hard skeleton around itself. When a polyp dies, its skeleton is left behind and a new polyp settles on top, growing the reef. Today, around two-thirds of coral reefs are at risk, as they are very sensitive to water temperature and pollution.

Up to 18 cm (7 in) long, the mirror butterflyfish feeds on coral polyps and small invertebrates.

Brain corals are among more than 3,000 species of stony corals. Each brain coral is a colony of thousands of tiny, identical living polyps.

This is a soft coral colony, made up of tiny polyps that do not build a hard skeleton. Polyps are food for reef fish and invertebrates.

Bright Shades

Many reef fish and invertebrates have brightly patterned bodies. For some, such as spotted trunkfish, the pattern warns other animals they are poisonous. Predators come to link that pattern with danger. Bright patterns are also useful for picking out other members of the same species for mating. For most reef species, their shades and patterns act as camouflage against the bright, sun-dappled reef.

This octopus is totally still as it waits for fish, crabs, or shrimp. In just a few seconds, it changes the shade and patterns on its skin to match the surrounding coral.

The emperor angelfish has bright blue and yellow stripes. It eats hard-to-chew sponges and algae with its large, strong jaws.

Copperband butterflyfish

COPPERBAND BUTTERFLYFISH

Length: 18 to 20 cm (7 to 8 in)

Range: Tropical coasts of the Indian and Pacific Oceans

Habitat: Coral reefs and rocky shores

Diet: Sea anenomes, worms, and mollusks

Conservation: Not at risk

Polar Waters

In winter, the surface of the Arctic Ocean and the sea surrounding Antarctica freezes. In summer, this sea ice melts and shrinks. Platforms of ice as thick as 1,000 m (3,300 ft), called ice shelves, extend into the ocean from the land. Sometimes, icebergs break off and float away.

Staying Warm

Animals that live in the Arctic and Southern Oceans must have special features to survive the cold. Mammals, such as seals and whales, have a thick layer of fat called blubber, which keeps in their body heat. They also have rounded bodies, with a smaller surface from which to lose heat. This has the same warming effect as huddling into a ball. Polar seabirds have a waterproof coat of tightly packed feathers.

Up to 2.3 m (7.5 ft) long, crabeater seals rest and mate on the sea ice around Antarctica.

Anti-Freeze Blood

Fish that live in the coldest waters need special protection to stop their blood from freezing. Antarctic icefish blood contains a special substance called glycoprotein. It disturbs the molecules in the blood, stopping them from joining together and freezing into ice.

The blood of an icefish is thin and see-though, which makes the fish transparent.

Narwhals are toothed whales that live in the Arctic Ocean, feeding on fish beneath the sea ice.

ARCTIC TERN

Length: 28 to 39 cm (11 to 15 in)

Range: Arctic and northern temperate coasts in northern summer; Southern Ocean and coasts in southern summer

Habitat: Coasts, grassland, and oceans

Diet: Small fish, crabs, and krill

Conservation: Population shrinking due to habitat loss and overfishing

Arctic tern

Narwhals live in groups of up to 20, joining together into groups of up to 1,000 in summer.

Male narwhals have a spiral tusk up to 3.1 m (10.2 ft) long. It is a tooth that grows from the left side of the mouth, through the lip.

Strange Fish

Boxfish, sunfish, porcupinefish, pufferfish, and triggerfish all belong to an order of bony fish called Tetraodontiformes (meaning "four teeth" in ancient Greek). Their unusual jaws form a beak shape, with tooth-like bones that are often used for crushing hard-shelled invertebrates.

Strange Bodies

For protection, most fish in this order are covered in bony plates, sharp spines, or tough skin. Their bodies are rigid, so they do not wriggle to swim. Instead, they move by waving their fins. These fish are also known for their strange body shapes, which may be nearly square (boxfish), round (porcupinefish), or flattened (sunfish and triggerfish).

A sunfish has perhaps the strangest-looking body of all fish. It ends behind the dorsal and anal fins, making the fish look as if it has lost its back half.

Puffing Up

Porcupinefish and pufferfish have a very effective defence when they are threatened by predators. They fill their stretchy stomachs with water, puffing the fish up until they are too big for most predators to swallow. In addition, they are covered by sharp spines. If this were not enough, pufferfish and some porcupinefish are also extremely poisonous.

The yellowspotted burrfish is a poisonous species of porcupinefish that lives on coral reefs. It can inflate (right) to nearly twice its normal size (left).

CLOWN TRIGGERFISH

Length: 40 to 50 cm (16 to 20 in)

Range: Tropical and subtropical coasts of the Indian and Pacific Oceans

Habitat: Coral reefs to depths of 75 m (250 ft)

Diet: Mollusks, crustaceans, and sea urchins

Conservation: Not known

Clown triggerfish

The tough horns make this fish harder to swallow. When threatened, the boxfish also releases poisonous mucus through its skin.

This boxfish eats algae, worms, crustaceans, and mollusks.

Jellyfish

Jellyfish are not fish but invertebrates related to sea anemones and corals. Adults have soft bodies with an umbrella-shaped "bell" and long tentacles. They swim by expanding and squeezing their bell, pushing water behind them.

Changing Body

A jellyfish starts life as a tiny, floating larva. When the larva finds a rock or other surface, it attaches to it and starts to grow into a polyp. Jellyfish polyps have a central mouth and tentacles for catching prey. After a few weeks or months, the polyp starts budding: its body breaks off into baby jellyfish, which swim away. These grow into adult jellyfish, called medusae. Medusae release eggs that grow into larvae.

Stinging Tentacles

Jellyfish tentacles have stinging cells that can stun or kill prey. Jellyfish may catch prey by trailing their tentacles behind them or sinking through the water with their tentacles spread wide. When prey is within reach, the tentacles direct it to the mouth, in the middle of the bell.

The golden jellyfish lives only in Jellyfish Lake, on the island of Eil Malk in the Pacific Ocean.

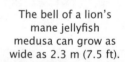

The bell of a lion's mane jellyfish medusa can grow as wide as 2.3 m (7.5 ft).

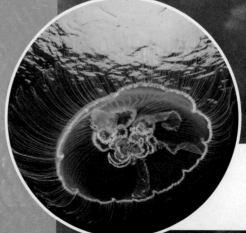

The moon jellyfish uses its tentacles to catch zooplankton.

24

The seawater lake is connected to the ocean by tunnels.

Thousands of golden jellyfish swim across the lake together every day.

CROWNED JELLYFISH

Length: 75 to 85 cm (30 to 33 in)

Range: Tropical Atlantic, Indian, and Pacific Oceans

Habitat: Open ocean

Diet: Plankton, algae, shrimp, and eggs

Conservation: Not at risk

Crowned jellyfish

Octopus and Squid

Octopus and squid are cephalopods, a group of 800 species that also includes nautilus and cuttlefish. Cephalopods have large heads and eyes, as well as arms or tentacles. Most of them have an ink sac, which can release a cloud of dark ink to confuse predators.

Moving Along

Octopus have eight arms covered with suckers, which they use to hold prey. Squid also have eight suckered arms, plus two long tentacles for grabbing. Octopus and squid can swim very fast by sucking in water, then pushing it out through a tube-shaped body part called a siphon. The animal moves in the opposite direction to the jet of water. Octopus can also crawl along the seafloor, while squid can swim gently by waving their fins.

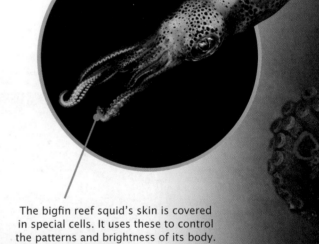

The bigfin reef squid's skin is covered in special cells. It uses these to control the patterns and brightness of its body.

Intelligent Invertebrates

Octopus signal to each other by changing the bright shades and patterns on their bodies, while Humboldt squid work together to capture prey. Several species of octopus, including blue-ringed octopus, use rocks and other objects to build dens.

SOUTHERN BOBTAIL SQUID

Length: 6 to 7 cm (2.4 to 2.8 in)

Range: Temperate coasts of Australia

Habitat: Seagrass meadows and sandy or muddy seafloors in shallow water

Diet: Shrimp and fish

Conservation: Not known

The southern bobtail squid is bioluminescent.

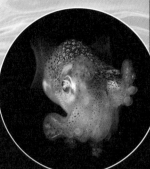

When the octopus feels threatened, the rings on its skin turn bright blue to frighten away predators.

This coconut octopus is walking on two "legs" as it carries a shell to hide inside.

Although all octopus have a venomous bite, only blue–ringed octopus make a venom so deadly it can kill humans.

Starfish

Also known as sea stars, starfish live on the ocean floor, from the shore to the depths. They are radially symmetrical, which means they usually have five equal parts arranged around their middles, like slices of a pie. Although most starfish have five arms, some have over fifty.

Creeping Predators

Starfish prey on other seafloor animals, particularly invertebrates. The starfish's mouth is in the middle of its underside. Many starfish can hunt prey much larger than their mouth. When they find prey, they move on top of it and push their stomach out through their mouth, inside-out. The stomach makes digestive fluids to break down the prey. After a while, the stomach and the partly digested prey are pulled inside.

This crown–of–thorns starfish has climbed onto coral and stuck out its stomach. It is turning the coral polyps to mush.

Tube Feet

The undersides of a starfish's arms have many tube-shaped growths called tube feet. Starfish creep slowly across the seafloor by waving their tube feet. These stick to surfaces, with one part of an arm attaching to a surface as another lets go.

The ochre starfish is often seen on wave-washed rocks. As well as being used for movement, its strong tube feet can open the shells of bivalves.

COMMON SUNSTAR

Length: 20 to 35 cm (8 to 14 in)

Range: Arctic and northern Atlantic and Pacific Oceans

Habitat: Rocky seafloor from shore rock pools to depths of 300 m (985 ft)

Diet: Starfish, sea urchins, bivalves, and sea squirts

Conservation: Population shrinking due to global warming

Common sunstar

Found in shallow waters of the Indian and Pacific Oceans, the red knob starfish grows to about 30 cm (12 in) wide.

If it loses one of its arms, this starfish can slowly grow a new one.

At the tip of each arm is an eyespot, which allows the starfish to see light and dark shapes.

Hunter Sharks

Sharks have skeletons made of bendy, lightweight cartilage rather than bone. Their mouths have several rows of teeth. These rows constantly move forward, then fall out and are replaced by the next. Most sharks are hunters, using their teeth for grabbing, biting, or crushing prey.

Shark Senses

Sharks have excellent senses of smell, sight, and hearing. Like most fish, sharks also have a sense system called the lateral line, which uses hairlike cells to feel water movements. In addition, sharks and other cartilaginous fish have sensing organs called ampullae of Lorenzini, which are jelly-filled pores in the skin. These detect electric fields, which are created by all living things when moving their muscles. A shark's ampullae can detect the beating heart of a completely still animal.

Growing up to 6.1 m (20 ft) long and reaching speeds of 56 km/h (35 mph), the great white shark is a fearsome predator. This adult is swallowing a whole seal.

Eye Protection

Many sharks have an extra, see-through eyelid called a nictitating membrane, which they close to protect their eyes when striking prey or being attacked. Some species, such as great white sharks, do not have a nictitating membrane, so they roll their eyeballs backward when lunging at prey.

This Caribbean reef shark has closed its nictitating membrane while holding a struggling lionfish.

SAND TIGER

Length: 2 to 3.2 m (6.6 to 10.5 ft)

Range: Subtropical and temperate Atlantic, Indian, and Pacific Oceans

Habitat: Coastal waters to depths of 190 m (620 ft)

Diet: Bony fish, rays, skates, and smaller sharks, such as smooth-hounds

Conservation: Population shrinking due to fishing

Sand tiger

As in other sharks, the hammerhead's gill slits are not covered. The slits are where water exits the body, after oxygen has been taken from it.

The scalloped hammerhead shark has eyes at either side of its hammer-shaped head. This means the shark can see 360 degrees, above and below.

This shark usually hunts fish such as sardines and mackerel.

Filter Feeder Sharks

Three species of sharks use a different method of feeding from their fierce relatives. Whale, megamouth, and basking sharks are filter feeders, straining tiny zooplankton and fish from the water. Although these sharks have hundreds of small teeth, they do not use them for eating.

Big Mouths

Filter feeding sharks have huge mouths. The largest of all is the whale shark's, which is 1.5 m (4.9 ft) wide. Filter feeders have two methods: either swimming forward with their mouth wide open so that water rushes inside, or sucking in mouthfuls of water. As the water flows out of the back of the mouth through the gills, filter pads in the gills act like sieves, catching tiny animals in the water.

Whale shark skin, which is up to 10 cm (4 in) thick, is marked with pale spots.

Whale sharks feed on small fish, squid, and zooplankton such as krill, eggs, and larvae.

The megamouth shark is so rare that no one knew it existed until 1976. Reaching 5.5 m (18 ft), it is the smallest of the filter feeding sharks.

WHALE SHARK

Length: 5.5 to 12.65 m (18 to 41.5 ft)

Range: Tropical and subtropical Atlantic, Indian, and Pacific Oceans

Habitat: Open ocean to depths of 1,800 m (5,900 ft)

Diet: Zooplankton, small fish, and squid

Conservation: Endangered due to fishing and collisions with boats

Whale shark

In one hour, a whale shark can filter more than 600 m³ (21,000 ft³) of water, swallowing 2 to 3 kg (4 to 7 lb) of food.

Threatened Sharks

Of the 440 species of sharks, over 70 are threatened with extinction, including whale and basking sharks. Every year, up to 100 million sharks are killed by fishermen, for food or sport. Most sharks give birth to a small number of live young, rather than releasing lots of eggs like many other fish. As a result, some shark species cannot reproduce fast enough to keep up their numbers.

The second largest species of shark, the basking shark is now protected by law in many countries.

33

Rays and Relatives

The giant oceanic manta ray can grow up to 7 m (23 ft) wide.

Rays—including skates, guitarfish, and sawfish—make up a group of fish called batoids. Like sharks, batoids have skeletons made of cartilage. They are flat bodied, and many species have extra-large, often wing-like, pectoral fins.

Flapping or Waving

Most batoids swim by moving their pectoral fins. This makes them different from sharks and most other fish, which power through the water using movements of their tail or body. Batoids such as manta rays and eagle rays have wide, pointed pectoral fins that they flap up and down, almost like birds. Batoids with rounder pectoral fins, such as electric rays, wave their fins, with the ruffling wave moving along the length of each fin.

The largest spotted eagle rays grow up to 5 m (16 ft) long, with a wingspan of up to 3 m (10 ft).

Electric Rays

The 69 species of electric rays make electricity in special organs on either side of their head. All living things, even humans, make tiny amounts of electricity as the body carries out its work, but electric rays make larger amounts and then store it, like in a battery. These rays can release a pulse of electricity to kill or stun their prey.

The leopard torpedo ray is a species of electric ray that uses electricity to capture fish, worms, and crustaceans.

Manta rays often visit "cleaning stations," where they pick up angelfish to eat the irritating parasites living on their body.

The cephalic fins channel water into the ray's open mouth, so it can filter feed on zooplankton.

BROWN GUITARFISH

Length: 80 to 100 cm (31 to 39 in)

Range: Tropical and subtropical coasts of the western Pacific Ocean

Habitat: Sandy and muddy seabeds to depths of 230 m (750 ft)

Diet: Fish, shrimp, and squid

Conservation: Not known

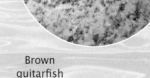

Brown guitarfish

Ocean Giants

Along with dolphins and porpoises, whales belong to the group of marine mammals called cetaceans. Cetaceans power through the water with their tail, steering with their two flippers. They spend their whole life in the water, but surface to breathe air through the blowholes on top of their head. There are 15 species of baleen whales.

Baleen

Baleen whales are named for the plates of bristly baleen in their mouth. Baleen is made of keratin, the same tough material that makes human nails. When they feed, baleen whales take in a mouthful of water, either by lunge-feeding (taking a huge gulp) or skim-feeding (swimming with an open mouth). The water is then released through the baleen plates, which trap small prey inside the mouth.

Some of the largest whales in the ocean have no teeth. This whale is showing its baleen plates, which grow in rows from the animal's upper jaw.

Whale Song

All whales make sounds to communicate with each other. During mating season, male baleen whales are known for their "songs" to attract females. Songs are made up of moans, chirps, and roars. Humpback whales have the most complex songs, lasting 10 to 20 minutes, which are repeated for hours. During each mating season, all humpback males in one region sing the same song, which changes from one season to the next. Sometimes, males in one region copy songs from other regions.

Humpback whales often move in small groups called pods, containing mothers and their calves, but they gather in larger groups during mating season.

SOUTHERN RIGHT WHALE

Length: 11 to 18 m (36 to 59 ft)

Range: Southern Ocean in southern summer; southern Atlantic, Indian, and Pacific Oceans in winter

Habitat: Open ocean in summer; coastlines in winter

Diet: Zooplankton and krill

Conservation: Population stable after huge losses due to hunting in previous centuries

Southern right whale

Barnacles often attach themselves to a humpback whale's skin.

The humpback whale, which reaches 16 m (52 ft) long, often leaps partway out of the water, called breaching.

The flippers have knobbles called tubercles. These are enlarged hair follicles, or roots from which hairs grow.

Dolphins

Dolphins are small whales, with a streamlined body for fast swimming and cone-shaped teeth for grasping prey. Dolphins make a wide range of sounds to communicate with each other, from clicks to whistles. Around 30 species of dolphins live in the oceans, with another four species living in rivers.

Living in a Pod

Dolphins are very sociable, living in pods that differ in size from species to species. A small pod may contain just a mother and her calves. Sometimes, family groups join together to number over a hundred dolphins—or even thousands where there is plenty of prey. Dolphins show strong bonds between friends and relatives. They often help weaker members of their pod, staying beside injured friends or helping them to the surface to breathe.

Up to 8 m (26 ft) long, orcas are the largest dolphins, but are sometimes called killer whales. Pods are led by the oldest female and contain her children and their children.

Acrobatics

Dolphins often leap above the water surface. Sometimes this is the quickest way, as it is easier to move through air than water. At other times, dolphins leap to see what is going on, to show off to each other, to shake parasites off their skin—or just to play. Dolphins sometimes play in other ways, by chasing each other or by tossing around objects.

Spinner dolphins are named for their habit of spinning around as they leap through the air.

Common bottlenose dolphins are 2 to 4 m (6.6 to 13 ft) long and live for 40 to 50 years.

This dolphin gets its name from its beak, which looks a little like the neck of a bottle.

These dolphins live in pods of around 15 animals. They often work together to capture shoals of fish.

STRIPED DOLPHIN

Length: 2 to 2.4 m (6.6 to 7.9 ft)

Range: Temperate to tropical Atlantic, Indian, and Pacific Oceans

Habitat: Usually deep oceans away from coasts

Diet: Fish, squid, octopus, krill, and other crustaceans

Conservation: Population shrinking due to tangling in nets, collisions with boats, and pollution

Striped dolphins

Polar Bears

The polar bear lives on and around the Arctic Ocean where it hunts the food it likes best: seals. These bears are born on land, but spend most of their life on the ice that covers the ocean surface, sometimes diving into the cold water. They have thick body fat and fur to keep them warm.

Born in a Den

Before the start of winter, when a female polar bear is pregnant, she digs a den in the snow, then climbs inside to rest. Snow soon covers the entrance, making it warm inside. Usually, the mother gives birth to two cubs, which start out completely blind. Although the mother has not eaten since entering her den, she feeds the cubs on her milk. In the spring, the family finally leaves the den and heads for the sea ice, where the mother hunts for prey for them all.

Cubs stay with their mother until they are about two and a half years old.

Hunting Seals

Polar bears usually catch seals when they come to holes in the ice to breathe. Bears use their powerful sense of smell to find a seal breathing hole, then crouch to wait. When a seal pops up, the bear drags it out with a clawed paw. Sometimes, polar bears creep close to seals that are resting on the ice, rushing forward in a final deadly attack.

Polar bears eat as many seals as possible from winter to summer. This allows them to store up energy for the late summer when the ice melts and hunting is difficult.

The bear can smell a seal at a distance of 1.6 km (1 mile).

The paws are large to help with swimming and to spread the bear's weight so it does not sink into snow or crash through thin sea ice.

A polar bear's coat appears white, but its hairs are actually transparent.

POLAR BEAR

Length: 1.8 to 3 m (5.9 to 9.8 ft)

Range: The coastal Arctic Ocean and surrounding land

Habitat: Sea ice, ocean, and land when sea ice melts in late summer.

Diet: Ringed, bearded, and other seals, plus bird eggs and dead walruses and whales

Conservation: Population at risk from global warming

Polar bear

Seals

There are 18 species of true seals. They have a streamlined body suited to swimming and deep diving, with two large back flippers for paddling and two smaller, clawed front flippers for steering. Since their back flippers cannot be pulled under the body for walking, true seals have to wriggle along on land.

Living for up to 35 years, the Atlantic seal is found in coastal waters of the northern Atlantic and Pacific Oceans.

Fast Parenting

True seals are so well suited to life in the ocean that they rarely go ashore. However, they do come to land, or onto sea ice, to give birth. A mother gives birth to only one pup, which she feeds on extremely high-fat milk for just a few days or weeks, depending on the species. Then the mother must return to the sea to hunt so she can survive. The pup lives off the fat it has built up until it has learned to hunt for itself.

A young Weddell seal yelps to tell its mother it is hungry for milk.

Elephant Seals

The largest seal is the southern elephant seal, with males reaching 6 m (19.7 ft) long. Elephant seals are named for the male's large snout, which looks a little like an elephant's trunk. The hollow, muscly snout acts a bit like a horn, making the male's roars even louder. Elephant seals are able to hold their breath for more than 100 minutes, longer than any mammal that is not a cetacean.

A seal's eyes can see well underwater and in air. When diving, a nictitating membrane, or see-through third eyelid, covers the eyeball for protection.

The male elephant seal roars to warn away other males, who might try to compete for females.

42

Like other true seals, which are also known as earless seals, the Atlantic seal has no ear flaps around the openings to its ears.

ATLANTIC SEAL

Length: 1.6 to 3.3 m (5.2 to 10.8 ft)

Range: Coastal northern Atlantic Ocean

Habitat: Coastal ocean, rocks, islands, and beaches

Diet: Fish, octopus, and lobsters

Conservation: Population growing since bans on hunting

Atlantic seal

Sea Turtles

From smallest to largest, the seven species of sea turtles are the Kemp's ridley, olive ridley, hawksbill, flatback, green, loggerhead, and leatherback. A sea turtle's large but streamlined body is protected by a shell divided into two parts: covering the back is the carapace, while covering the underside is the plastron.

Nesting on a Beach

At the start of mating season, sea turtles swim from their feeding areas to their coastal mating areas, which may be thousands of kilometres away. When a female is ready to lay her eggs, she climbs onto the beach, usually at night, and digs a hole in the sand using her back flippers. She lays a clutch of soft-shelled eggs, covers them with smoothed sand to disguise the spot, then returns to the sea. After 50 to 60 days, female babies hatch from eggs that were kept warmer, while males hatch from cooler eggs.

Female loggerhead turtles always nest on the beach where they were born. They lay around 100 eggs in each nest, making about four nests per season. Just a handful of babies will survive to adulthood.

This olive ridley turtle is swimming through plastic rubbish, which it might mistake for food, clogging its stomach.

At Risk

Sea turtles are among the world's most threatened animals. The Kemp's ridley and hawksbill turtles are "critically endangered," while the green turtle is "endangered." The other species, apart from the flatback, are "vulnerable," which means they will become endangered if care is not taken. Threats faced by sea turtles include damage to their nesting beaches, water pollution, tangling in fishing nets, and rising sea temperatures.

FLATBACK TURTLE

Length: 76 to 100 cm (30 to 39 in)

Range: Coastal waters of Australia and New Guinea, in the Indian and Pacific Oceans

Habitat: Tropical and subtropical waters with soft beds, at depths up to 60 m (200 ft)

Diet: Soft coral, shrimp, jellyfish, and sea cucumbers

Conservation: At risk from habitat damage and pollution

A flatback turtle hatchling

The mouth is sharp and hooked, like a beak, which makes it ideal for eating tough sea sponges, algae, and jellyfish.

The carapace is made up of 13 overlapping bony plates called scutes.

Growing to around 114 cm (45 in) long, the hawksbill lives mainly on tropical coral reefs in the Atlantic, Indian, and Pacific Oceans.

Penguins

A penguin's small wings, which are shaped like a dolphin's flippers, cannot lift it into the air at all. These seabirds spend three-quarters of their life swimming in the ocean, with most species living in the cold waters of the southern hemisphere. Their blubber and thick, waterproof feathers keep them warm.

Hunters

Penguins dive for fish, squid, and krill. The largest species, such as the 110 cm/43 in-tall emperor penguin, can dive as deep as 565 m (1,855 ft) and stay underwater for up to 22 minutes. Smaller species, such as the little penguin that is only 33 cm (13 in) tall, cannot swim as fast or hold their breath so long, and find their food near the surface. All penguins catch prey in their beak and swallow it whole as they swim.

When the gentoo penguin is swimming, its movements look similar to a bird flying through the air. When the gentoo comes ashore, it is on Antarctica or islands in the far southern seas.

Getting Together

Penguins are sociable birds: they hunt, sleep on the water surface, and nest with other penguins. Many species come to land only to mate, when they gather in large and loud colonies. Penguins often return to the same mate year after year. However, females desert their mate if he no longer seems healthy. A large body size, a deep call, and bright feathers are signs of fitness. In most species, males and females share the exhausting care of their eggs and young chicks.

The world's largest penguin colony is on Zavodovskiy Island, in the Southern Ocean. It is home to 1.2 million chinstrap (pictured) and macaroni penguins.

Up to 1 m (3.3 ft) tall, the king penguin gathers to mate on islands in the cold southern oceans.

Parents take turns warming their egg, balancing it on their feet and tucked inside a pouch of skin.

Most penguins lay two eggs, but the king penguin lays only one, which takes 55 days to hatch.

SOUTHERN ROCKHOPPER PENGUIN

Length: 45 to 58 cm (18 to 23 in)

Range: Southern Atlantic, Indian, and Pacific Oceans

Habitat: Open ocean; nests on rocky islands and coasts

Diet: Krill, fish, squid, and octopus

Conservation: Population shrinking due to climate change, overfishing, and oil spills

Southern rockhopper penguin

Glossary

ALGAE
Simple plants and plantlike chromists that usually live in and around water, such as seaweeds

ARTHROPOD
An invertebrate with a hard covering, or exoskeleton, and jointed legs, such as an insect or crab.

BACTERIA
Microscopic living things with one simple cell.

BIOLUMINESCENT
Able to make its own light.

BLOOD VESSEL
A tube that carries blood through an animal's body.

CAMOUFLAGE
Different ways in which an animal makes itself less visible in its habitat.

CHROMIST
A living thing that makes its food from sunlight and has just one type of complex cell.

CURRENT
A stream of water that flows through the ocean.

DORSAL FIN
A fin on the back of a fish or a cetacean.

FILTER FEEDING
Straining food from the water using comb- or net-like body parts.

FIN
A body part that juts from the body of fish and some other water-living animals, helping them swim.

HABITAT
The natural home of an animal, plant, or other living thing.

HEMISPHERE
Half of the planet, such as the northern or southern half on either side of the equator.

INVERTEBRATE
An animal without a backbone, such as a crab, squid, or insect.

LARVA
A young stage in the life cycle of some invertebrates, during which the animal looks very different from its adult form.

MAMMAL
An animal that grows hair at some point in its life and feeds its young on milk, such as a whale or human.

MICROORGANISM
A living thing that is so small it can be seen only with a microscope.

MINERAL
A solid that forms in the ground or in water.

MOLLUSK
An invertebrate with a soft body and sometimes a hard shell, such as a slug, snail, clam, or octopus.

ORGAN
A body part that does a particular job, such as the heart or brain.

PECTORAL FIN
One of a pair of fins on either side of a fish, just behind its head.

PHOTOSYNTHESIS
The process of using sunlight to make food energy.

PHYTOPLANKTON
Tiny drifting plants, chromists, and some bacteria that make food from sunlight.

POLYP
The sessile, or non-moving, life stage of invertebrates such as corals.

REPTILE
An animal with a dry, scaly skin that usually lays eggs on land.

SPECIES
A group of living things that look similar and can mate together.

TIDE
The rising and falling of the ocean at the shore, caused by the pull of the Moon's gravity on the water.

TROPICAL
In the area around the equator, where the water is warm all year.

ZOOPLANKTON
Tiny animals, eggs, and larvae that drift through the water.